Dear Parents, Grandparents and Educators,

Do you remember being told to go outside and play as a child? Without realizing it, our parents gave us the greatest gift of all, freedom to experience the great outdoors where our imagination ran wild and our stress and unneeded calories melted away.

Today's children are held captive by our fears and electronic devices. Spending more than 7 ½ hours a day consuming media, these "digital natives" often spend less than 1 hour a week on unstructured recreation. As a society, we have a moral and ethical obligation to give the natural world back to our children.

Every child needs time in a natural setting. The American Academy of Pediatrics recommends sixty minutes of daily unstructured free play as essential to children's physical and mental health. The worldwide initiative to reconnect children with the natural world is making a difference. The International Union for Conservation of Nature in 2012 recognized "Children have a human right to a connection to the natural world and to a healthy world."

Recent scientific research identifies strong correlations between experiences in nature and children's ability to learn and cope. Schools with environmental education programs score higher on standardized tests in math, reading, writing and listening. The National Wildlife Federation notes Cal Tech's Jet Propulsion Lab interviews all candidates about their play experiences as children, because they've found a direct correlation between hands- on play and superior problem solving skills.

National Garden Clubs, Inc. encourages you to read and discuss The Frightened Frog with your children. Even better, take them on a quest to find an egg mass, tadpoles, frogs and other amphibians. Become an environmental hero! Sit and listen while enjoying the mystery and magnificence of the natural world with the most important people anywhere, our children.

As parents, grandparents, and educators, we have a pivotal role in the experiences of the future stewards of the natural world. Now is not the time to hesitate but to leap into action.

Sandra H. Robinson
President 2015-2017
National Garden Clubs, Inc.

For information on National Garden Clubs, Inc., our Youth projects and scholarship program please visit www.gardenclub.org.

Imagine a spring with no "ribbitt, ribbitt", no deep croak of a bullfrog, or squeak of a tree frog. It is not just a supposition; it is fast becoming a reality all over the world. The frogs that little boys often put in pockets to later scare little sisters or the frogs that were part of jumping contests in state fairs are rapidly disappearing worldwide.

Adults can understand the threats to wildlife food chains. We know the idea of lost genomes that leave holes in the hereditary patterns of amphibians. We understand they are still finding examples of amphibians that have never been identified and we know that frogs, toads and salamanders have poisonous defenses and chemicals that might lead to medical breakthroughs. However, children do not always connect with academic reasons for loss and preservation. Children are far more likely to "care" about the loss of a frog that might become a prince charming or a magical pet to Neville Longbottom in Harry Potter or maybe "Mister Toad" in *The Mister Toad of Toad Hall.*

The loss of frogs can best be related to young children through their love of nature and their caring nurture in dealing with animals. We recognize their desire to help in a way that translates to methods of preservation or stewardship. Adults should point out the beautiful and interesting world around them while reminding the child there is a need for their care to maintain the wonderful diversity,

Children can understand the differences in quality of habitats and environments.

- They can be shown the places that are not hospitable to amphibians and ones that allow the frogs and toad to flourish.

- They can be told about the frog's temperature being controlled by ambient temperature.

- Healthy water sources are necessary for frogs and tadpoles. Children can be shown the natural habitat that leads to healthy amphibians.

- Children can view egg masses to understand how the strong ultraviolet sunlight causes problems for developing embryos, as does fungus and viruses.

- It is easy to describe the porous skin of an amphibian while viewing one. This will help them understand how easily poisons and diseases in the environment can impact a frog.

Continued on next page

- Tadpoles have been used in classrooms for years to demonstrate the stages of a developing frog. A great lesson at the end of this process is to release the frog into a suitable habitat. Children feel pride in helping this creature survive and thrive.

- Tadpoles are often found in puddles that are drying up. The frogs to be can be rescued and moved. Children understand the concept of stewardship even when the word is too big for them.

- Immersing young people in nature helps them recognize the needs and provides them with alternative solutions they understand.
    Surround them with pictures, stories, games and other representatives of the amphibians, the children will become endeared to the animals. Encourage parents and educators to dialogue with children about the problems facing frogs and toads.

- Incorporate the animals in playtime through coloring, cut outs of toads and frogs, making toad houses, and exercise by hopping like a frog.

The children will incorporate ideas into their culture. You can awe a young child with stories of the foot long Goliath frog, the tiny Brazilian Gold tree frog or even the Cricket frog that can jump forty times its length. There are sad stories all over the world of amphibians being lost to habitat destruction or climate change. You can help them study the Golden Frog extinction due to habitat destruction and discuss the possible things that might lead to saving frogs in the future.

Children are like frogs, they can absorb from their environment easily. We have to create a positive kind of environment where stewardship doesn't have to be defined, it is understood. The beauty of our world depends on it.

Lynn White
Science Professor/Advisor

The Frightened Frog

There's more to frogs than you might suppose,
I'm frightened because we have many woes.
Pesticides, diseases, habitat loss, and pollution
Where, oh where do we find the solution?

Amphibian, I am, born in the
water, lives on the land,
A life that may be hard for
humans to understand.
I began life in an egg mass and
it was my goal
to escape that egg mass and
become a tadpole.

Frogs have been around since the dinosaur,
What frightened me then was to hear them roar.
I hopped around and only wished
Not to be stepped on and not to get squished.

But now I am facing my biggest trial
I'm just hoping we can exist for awhile.
For our numbers are reaching all-time lows
And we'll soon be extinct if it's up to our foes.

Some people catch us to eat our legs.
We plead with them not to, oh no, we beg.
If you see someone searching for a frog to gig,
Tell them to leave us alone - let us grow big.

Bulldozers come and take away our ponds
And then we have no place in which to spawn.
We like to jump in the water and play.
We hide under lily pads so we're
nobody's prey.

People often spray pesticides to kill weeds and plants.
"Use safer ways, not pesticides",
every frog rants.
Pesticides go into our ponds and into our skin
And once we are poisoned we're never well again.

The changing climate has dried up our streams, Earth's weather can hurt us, especially the extremes.

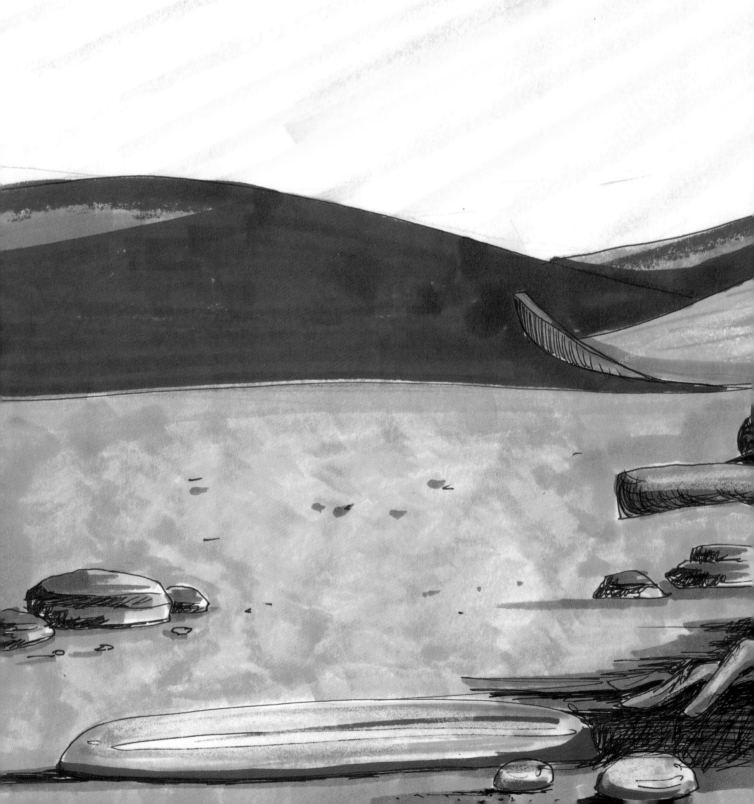

Also we've met foreign fish that we thought wanted to greet us. But the truth be told they only wanted to eat us.

Try not to touch us and move us around,
It can kill us with diseases that quickly abound.
Many of us are an endangered species that's for sure,
Something must be done to help us endure.

We eat bugs and mosquitoes
that make humans ill,
Now, don't you think that's
an important skill?
As tadpoles we eat algae to
keep our water clear
We frogs are so helpful,
so please keep us near.

Without all the frogs nobody can win,
Human health is improved when they
study our skin.
We are part of the ecosystem
that needs to survive
So please do your part to
help keep frogs alive.

A kiss from a princess, we become their prince charming,
A fairy tale we've heard that's not really alarming.
But if the story couldn't end with a happily ever after,
There would be no more croaking, there would be no
more laughter.

5 MILLION MORE!

I look forward to spending two million more years
With my human friends and amphibian peers.
So you see there's more to frogs than you might suppose
And now this brings my story to a close.

FUN FROG FACTS

A group of frogs is called an army

Frogs stalk their prey like cats

Frogs can see forwards, sideways and upwards all at the same time

Frogs never close their eyes even when they sleep

Frogs squash their eyeballs down to swallow their food

Most frogs have small teeth around the upper edge of their jaw

Frogs completely shed their skin about once a week and they usually eat it

Instead of drinking water frogs soak it into their body through their skin

Frogs ears are connected to their lungs

Some frogs make so much noise that they can be heard for miles

Frogs are one of the best leapers on the planet

Frogs hibernate in the wintertime

Albino frogs are a fairly common occurrence with frogs

Some frogs can change colors to avoid predators

Scientist believe the frog's ability to jump helped it escape being eaten by dinosaurs

It was discovered on a space mission that a frog can throw up

In Japan, frogs are symbols of Good Luck

You get warts from human viruses, not from frogs and toads

All toads are frogs but not all frogs are toads

The fear of frogs is called Ranidaphobia

Frogs in the environment are a true sign of a well balanced ecosystem

It is unknown how many frogs have actually turned into princes after being kissed by a princess...

References:

allaboutfrogs.org
funfunnyfacts.com

What sound does a frog make in YOUR language? Here is a list of some of the different ways people think frogs sound around the world!

Afrikaans: kwaak-kwaak

Arabic (Algeria): gar gar

Catalan: cru-cru

Chinese (Mandarin): guo guo

Dutch: kwak kwak

English (USA): ribbit

English (GB): croak

Finnish: kvak kvak

French: coa-coa

German: quaak, quaak

Hebrew: kwa kwa

Hungarian: bre-ke-ke

Italian: cra cra

Japanese: kerokero

Korean: gaegool-gae-gool

Russian: kva-kva

Spanish (Spain): cru-cru

Spanish (Argentina): berp

Spanish (Peru): croac, croac

Swedish: kvack

Thai: ob ob (with high tone)

Turkish: vrak vrak

Ukrainian: kwa-kwa

Reference:

allaboutfrogs.org

GLOSSARY

amphibian – animal that is able to live both on land and in water such as frogs and salamanders

ecosystem – a system of living things living in nature

endangered – is in danger

extinct – no longer alive

gig – a pronged spear for catching fish

habitat – place to live

mass – a group; egg mass is a group of eggs

pesticides – substance used to destroy pest, usually poisonous

pollution – to mess up, to make impure

prey – something hunted by another animal

spawn – to lay eggs

tadpole – a baby frog which has a big head and tail and lives only in the water

Brenda Moore resides in Oak Hill, WV and is a graduate of West Virginia University and a proud mountaineer. She is the past president of West Virginia Garden Club. She serves on the National Garden Club board as Membership Committee Chairman, President's Special Project committee member, The Frightened Frog Chairman, and as a member of the Future Planning Committee. She married a 'Prince', Ron, without having to kiss a frog. She is mother to Rebekah and Andy, mother-in-law to Andy and Emily and grandmother to seven frog-loving grandsons, Ethan, Micah, Ben, Noah, Caleb, Joshua and Asher.

Jean Ohlmann, Chemical Engineer, art minor and english major, found her passion in garden club. She has served as chairman of the Flower Show Schools Committee, Gardening Studies School Committee as well as heading most positions on those committees. She currently serves as a member of the Vision of Beauty Calendar Committee. Jean lives in Louisville Kentucky and serves as the garden club representative on the Yew Dell Gardens Education Committee. Jean is thankful for the path National Garden Clubs has given her to wander and has found a new adventure with The Frightened Frog.

Emily Lackey grew up in Campbellsville, Kentucky. Her art career began in 6th grade when she designed t-shirts for the class. She graduated with a degree in art from Georgetown College on a tennis and art scholarship. As a mother Emily realizes the importance of reading and outdoor connections for children. The Frightened Frog showcases her love of painting BIG. Emily lives in Chattanooga, Tennessee with her husband Ryan, son Grant, and daughter Carson.

List of Committee Members
The Frightened Frog

Sandra H. Robinson
NGC President
2015-2017

Kay Fisher
Chairman, President's Special Project

Ann Fiel
Vice Chairman, President's Special Project

Brenda Moore
Chairman, The Frightened Frog
Author

Jean Ohlmann
Vice Chairman, The Frightened Frog
Author

Becky Hassebroek
Habitat Advisor

Lynn White
Science Professor/Advisor